The Impressionist Landscape
from Corot to van Gogh

Masterworks from the Museum of Fine Arts, Boston

BELLAGIO GALLERY OF FINE ART

Published by Authentic Press L.L.C.
945 Foch St., Fort Worth, TX 76107

on the occasion of the exhibition

**The Impressionist Landscape
from Corot to van Gogh**
Masterworks from the Museum of Fine Arts, Boston

Bellagio Gallery of Fine Art, Las Vegas
June 10, 2005 to January 8, 2006

Catalogue © 2005 PaperBall Las Vegas, L.L.C.
Photographs © 2005 Museum of Fine Arts, Boston

Front cover:

Design and production by Derrick Saunders
Plywoodskyscraper Studios, Inc.

Text by Matthew D. Hileman

ISBN: 0-9769649-0-2
Printed in U.S.A.

Right:
Johann Barthold Jongkind, Dutch, 1819–1891
Harbor by Moonlight
1871
Oil on canvas
13 3/8 x 18 1/8 inches
The Henry C. and Martha B. Angell Collection

Previous page:
Jean-Baptiste-Camille Corot, French, 1796–1875
Morning near Beauvais
about 1855–65
Oil on canvas
14 1/8 x 16 3/8 inches
Juliana Cheney Edwards Collection

The Impressionist Landscape
from Corot to van Gogh

Masterworks from the Museum of Fine Arts, Boston

BELLAGIO GALLERY OF FINE ART

Foreword

Following the extraordinary success of the exhibition *Claude Monet: Masterworks from the Museum of Fine Arts, Boston* at the Bellagio Gallery of Fine Art, we take great pleasure in presenting this exhibition, *The Impressionist Landscape from Corot to van Gogh*, entirely drawn from the MFA's collections. We are once again proud to share our nineteenth-century French paintings with a wide variety of audiences—including not only people from all over the world who visit Las Vegas, but also the many residents of the city who can take pleasure in seeing these works over and over again.

Bostonians were among the most fervent collectors of French art in the 1850s and 1860s, when paintings by Corot, Millet, and Rousseau were vanguard contemporary art. As the decades went on, Boston collectors moved from their fascination with the art of the Barbizon School to a new engagement with Impressionism, eagerly seeking out works by Monet, Renoir, Pissarro, and others.

The reverence for nature that is a key element in the philosophical movements that grew up in Boston in the middle years of the nineteenth century found its artistic expression in these paintings— whether by the Realists of the 1850s and 1860s or by the Impressionists in the last quarter of the century. Visitors to *The Impressionist Landscape from Corot to van Gogh* will sense that love of nature again and again as they look at the paintings on view here—in both the private, freely-painted sketches that try to capture an "impression" and the more highly-finished compositions intended for public exhibition.

We hope that all who come to see these paintings will take pleasure in that sensation. It is the surest proof that artistic expression can conquer time and place, taking us from the American west in the early twenty-first century to stand at the side of artists in the fields and forests of France more than one hundred years ago.

Malcolm Rogers
Ann and Graham Gund Director
Museum of Fine Arts, Boston

Claude Monet, French, 1840–1926
Flower Beds at Vétheuil
1881
Oil on canvas
44 1/8 x 33 7/8 inches
The John Pickering Lyman Collection
Gift of Miss Theodora Lyman

Introduction

Less than a decade ago the very notion of fine art in Las Vegas was incredulous to the world outside of the city. Despite a burgeoning art museum, whose origins began in the 1950s, it seemed to many unlikely that the city would ever become a cosmopolitan destination with an art space that would exhibit masterpieces from some of the world's finest public and private collections. It has now been nearly seven years since the opening of Bellagio and the realization of a gallery that has welcomed nearly three million visitors eager to experience exhibitions drawn from collections in America, Europe, and as far away as Russia.

In 2004, the Bellagio Gallery of Fine Art embarked on what was then its most ambitious project to date–to collaborate with one of America's leading art institutions to mount a single-venue exhibition of paintings by the nineteenth-century French Impressionist, Claude Monet. The resulting collaboration, *Claude Monet: Masterworks from the Museum of Fine Arts, Boston*, drew nearly 450,000 visitors from around the globe.

We are pleased and delighted to be once again working with the venerable Museum of Fine Arts, Boston to draw yet another exhibition from their collection of nineteenth-century French masterpieces, considered one of the finest outside France. Through thirty-four works, *The Impressionist Landscape from Corot to van Gogh* explores the origins of Impressionism and the art of landscape painting, which reached its zenith in the second half of the nineteenth century.

We would like to thank Malcolm Rogers, Ann and Graham Gund Director and the Board of Trustees of the Museum of Fine Arts, Boston without whose generous support this exhibition could not have been possible. Special thanks also to Katie Getchell, George Shackelford, Jennifer Bose, Debra LaKind, Dawn Griffin, Kelly Gifford, Kim Pashko, Rhona MacBeth, Jean Woodward, and Irene Konefal of the Museum of Fine Arts, Boston, and Neil Cantor, Matthew Hileman and the entire staff of the Bellagio Gallery of Fine Art for their invaluable assistance with this exhibition.

Marc and Andrea Glimcher
Chairman and President
Bellagio Gallery of Fine Art

Jean-François Millet, French, 1814–1875
Washerwomen
about 1855
Oil on canvas
17 1/8 x 21 1/8 inches
Gift of Mrs. Martin Brimmer

The Impressionist Landscape from Corot to van Gogh

Masterworks from the Museum of Fine Arts, Boston

Contents

Vincent van Gogh, Dutch, 1853–1890
Houses at Auvers
1890
Oil on canvas
29 3/4 x 24 3/8 inches
Bequest of John T. Spaulding

Louis-Eugène Boudin
French, 1824–1898

From his early childhood in Honfleur on the Normandy coast, Eugène Boudin became intimately acquainted with the light and atmosphere of the sea. His father was a sea captain and for a time Boudin worked as a cabin boy on his father's steamer, which plied the coast between Honfleur and Le Havre. As a young man, Boudin worked as an apprentice to a stationer and printer in Le Havre who displayed paintings by visiting artists. It was there that he came into contact with Jean-François Millet and Constant Troyon. He eventually traveled to Paris where he met members of the Barbizon School, including Camille Corot and Charles-François Daubigny. It was from them that he would learn the benefit of traveling and painting directly from nature.

Harbor at Honfleur
1865
Oil on paper mounted on panel
8 x 10 1/2 inches
Anonymous gift

By 1858 Boudin was an established artist. At an exhibition held that year in Le Havre, he met the young Claude Monet. He encouraged Monet to take up painting and stressed the importance of working in the open air. Monet and Boudin would remain lifelong friends and the influence of Boudin's vigorous brushwork is evident in Monet's work. Although Boudin never considered himself a radical or an innovator, it was his ability to capture in paint the essence of atmosphere and light that would have the most impact on Monet and the development of Impressionism.

Left:
Ships at Le Havre
1887
Oil on panel
13 3/4 x 10 3/8 inches
Gift of Miss Amelia Peabody

Right:
Figures on the Beach
1893
Oil on canvas
14 3/8 x 23 1/4 inches
Bequest of William A. Coolidge

Paul Cézanne
French, 1839–1906

Paul Cézanne was born into an affluent family in the southern French town of Aix-en-Provence. For a time he studied law but quickly abandoned the profession for a career as an artist. In the early years of his career, Cézanne traveled often between Aix and Paris. It was in Paris, however, at the Académie Suisse, that he came into contact with Monet, Renoir, and Pissarro. Pissarro, who was nearly ten years older than the other Impressionists, played an instrumental role in the development of Cézanne's signature style. He introduced Cézanne to painting out-of-doors and to applying paint in a manner that utilized bold, broken strokes of color.

Cézanne showed his work in only two of the Impressionist exhibitions. For him, Impressionism lacked the grandeur of the Old Masters. He set out to develop his own style of painting and eventually abandoned the Impressionists and public life to work exclusively in his studio and the countryside around his native Aix. He would not begin to receive wide public acceptance for his work until much later in life. At the age of 56 he had his first solo exhibition; his art was embraced by a new generation of artists who would later shape the art of the twentieth century. After his death, more and more artists looked to Cézanne's work as a source of inspiration. Pablo Picasso called him "the father of us all."

The Pond
about 1877–79
Oil on canvas
18 1/2 x 22 1/8 inches
Tompkins Collection

Jean-Baptiste-Camille Corot
French, 1796–1875

In the early part of the nineteenth century, an artist's education was not considered complete without a trip to Italy. For centuries Italian art had served as a well of inspiration for young artists who traveled from all over Europe to study the works of the great masters. The Italian countryside too, dotted with classical ruins and bathed in luminous light, would inspire generations of artists to paint romantic landscapes both real and imagined.

Using money he received from an inheritance and relying on the generosity of his family, Camille Corot traveled to Italy in the autumn of 1825 and remained there until the summer of 1828. He had received some formal training in Paris in the studio of Achille Etna Michallon, who preached the virtue of making sketches and oil studies directly from the chosen motif. In Italy, Corot did just that and developed a formula for making landscape sketches that could be translated in the studio into larger finished canvases for exhibition. Corot's sensitively rendered landscapes often include peasants, gypsies, or imaginary figures inspired by classical mythology. However, it was his handling of light and, more importantly, his consummate love of traveling great distances to work directly from nature that would influence the next generation of artists would who become known as the Impressionists.

Twilight
1845–60
Oil on canvas
19 3/4 x 14 5/8 inches
Bequest of Mrs. Henry Lee Higginson, Sr.,
in memory of her husband

Morning near Beauvais
about 1855–65
Oil on canvas
14 1/8 x 16 3/8 inches
Juliana Cheney Edwards Collection

Corot

Left:
Young Woman Weaving a Wreath of Flowers
about 1866–70
Oil on canvas
27 5/8 x 18 1/2 inches
Bequest of David P. Kimball in memory of his wife,
Clara Bertram Kimball

Right:
Bacchanal at the Spring: Souvenir of Marly-le-Roi
1872
Oil on canvas
32 3/8 x 26 1/8 inches
Robert Dawson Evans Collection

Charles-François Daubigny
French, 1817–1878

The Barbizon School was an informal movement consisting of a group of artists who worked in the countryside around the French town of Barbizon. This group included Théodore Rousseau, Constant Troyon, and Charles-François Daubigny. The Barbizon School painters were the precursors of the Impressionists as they dedicated themselves to painting landscapes inspired by humble sites and subjects.

Daubigny was the son of a landscape painter who had studied with Camille Corot's first teacher. Like Corot, Daubigny traveled to Italy, visiting many of the same towns and surrounding countryside before returning to Paris to study in the studio of the figure painter Paul Delaroche. Daubigny was one of the first artists to experiment with capturing the fleeting effects of nature on canvas. He had a particular interest in rendering the vivid and transitory atmosphere of dawn, twilight, and moonlight using a loose brushstroke that was derided by critics for giving his paintings an unfinished appearance.

Daubigny's influence on the Impressionist movement is undeniable. Among his pupils were Eugène Boudin and Johann Barthold Jongkind. He later met Monet and Pissarro and introduced them to his art dealer, Paul Durand-Ruel, who would become one of the most important promoters of the Impressionist group.

Château-Gaillard at Sunset
about 1873
Oil on canvas
15 x 27 inches
Gift of Mrs. Josiah Bradlee

François-Louis Français
French, 1814–1897

François-Louis Français began his career in Paris as a printmaker providing illustrations for books, including novels by Honoré de Balzac and George Sand. In 1834, he traveled to Barbizon to paint in the Forest of Fontainebleau. There he met Camille Corot. He began exhibiting at the Salon in 1837 and continued to show both paintings and lithographs there until 1896. His landscapes record a lifetime of travels that included trips throughout France and Italy. He often worked with Corot and Constant Troyon and after 1850 frequented Honfleur, where he painted with Eugène Boudin and Johann Barthold Jongkind. Français remained much sought after throughout his lifetime and enjoyed a successful career. He received numerous awards including induction into the Legion of Honor.

Sunset
1878
Oil on canvas
18 9/16 x 22 3/16 inches
Bequest of Ernest Wadsworth Longfellow

Paul Gauguin
French, 1848–1903

As a child, Paul Gauguin lived for a time on his great-uncle's estate in Lima, Peru. At 17, he joined the merchant marines and spent six years traveling the world. Before becoming a painter, Gauguin was a successful stockbroker at a Parisian bank. This afforded him a substantial income, which allowed him to collect paintings. He visited the first Impressionist exhibition in 1874 and later met Camille Pissarro, who encouraged him to buy works by the Impressionists. Pissarro, the consummate mentor, also encouraged Gauguin to paint. Following the stock market crash of 1882, Gauguin lost his job and was forced to sell his art collection. Nonetheless, he believed he could support his family with his painting.

Gauguin was a highly experimental artist who rejected naturalism in favor of symbolism and arbitrary color. He received little commercial success during his lifetime, and only a few critics recognized the importance of his work. During the 1880s he lived in rural French villages, and in the middle years of the decade moved to Brittany, painting in the coastal towns of Pont-Aven and Le Pouldu. The collaboration between Gauguin and Vincent van Gogh in Arles in 1888 is one of the most famous episodes in the history of art. In 1891, Gauguin left France for Tahiti. He returned to Paris for a brief period between 1893 and 1895 but, after receiving little recognition for his paintings of Tahitian subjects, he left Europe and his family permanently in the winter of 1895. Gauguin spent the last years of his life on the remote island of Hiva Oa in the Marquesas. He died there alone and impoverished, never to realize the acclaim he would later receive for his work or the influence it would have on the art of the twentieth century.

Forest Interior (Sous Bois)
1884
Oil on canvas
21 7/8 x 18 1/8 inches
Gift of Laurence K. and Lorna J. Marshall

Vincent van Gogh
Dutch, 1853–1890

Vincent van Gogh, the son of a minister, had very little formal training as an artist. After attempting several professions, he took up the life of the artist in 1880. He traveled across northern Europe before joining his brother Theo in Paris in 1886. It was there that he met members of the Impressionist group and a new generation of progressive painters such as Paul Signac, Georges Seurat, Henri de Toulouse-Lautrec, and Paul Gauguin. The excitement of the capital however proved to be too much for van Gogh's delicate mental state and in 1888 he moved to Arles in the south of France. It was in December of that year, while living with Gauguin, that van Gogh had a breakdown. After a violent argument with Gauguin he cut off part of his left ear. The dramatic incident marked the end of van Gogh's collaboration with Gauguin and the beginning of a series of mental breakdowns that would eventually lead to his suicide in 1890.

Enclosed Field with Ploughman
October 1889
Oil on canvas
21 1/4 x 25 3/4 inches
Bequest of William A. Coolidge

In the spring of the following year, van Gogh agreed to enter an asylum in the town of St. Rémy, near Arles. The hospital was housed in an ancient monastery with a pleasant garden that became the subject of a number of van Gogh's canvases. Under the care of doctors, he was given a single room and allowed to use a small room in the basement as a studio. From his window, which was reinforced with iron bars, van Gogh had a view of a nearby wheat field. Later that spring, his spirits improved and encouraged by favorable weather, he began making day trips outside of the hospital. Rising at six and accompanied by a guardian, he roamed the countryside painting the fields and hillsides. After a year in St. Rémy, van Gogh moved to Auvers, a town just north of Paris. He continued to work feverishly until his death in July 1890. The highly expressive works from this period are considered among his finest.

Houses at Auvers
1890
Oil on canvas
29 3/4 x 24 3/8 inches
Bequest of John T. Spaulding

Johann Barthold Jongkind
Dutch, 1819–1891

Johann Barthold Jongkind was a Dutch painter who, along with Eugène Boudin, spent his career translating into paint the fleeting atmosphere of the sea. He traveled to Paris from Amsterdam in 1846 to study art, living on a stipend awarded by the Dutch government. Jongkind remained in Paris for nearly the remainder of his life but traveled often to the Normandy coast, where he met Boudin and Claude Monet. Jongkind and Boudin both encouraged the young Monet, playing an instrumental role in his formative years as an artist.

Paintings of tall sailing ships moored in harbors were typical of Dutch Old Masters, but Jongkind's handling of the time-honored subject was bold and modern. It was his free, painterly style, which combined small dashes of paint with bold strokes of color that would influence the development of Impressionism as a movement. However, unlike Boudin and Monet, Jongkind did not work out-of-doors preferring to work in his studio from pencil sketches and watercolors taken from nature.

Harbor Scene in Holland
1868
Oil on canvas
16 1/2 x 22 inches
Gift of Count Cecil Pecci-Blunt

Right:
Harbor by Moonlight
1871
Oil on canvas
13 3/8 x 18 1/8 inches
The Henry C. and Martha B. Angell Collection

Jean-François Millet
French, 1814–1875

Jean-François Millet is often associated with the Barbizon School and the origins of Impressionism. His style and his subject matter, however, were distinctly Realist. Instead of simply capturing the essence of nature, his mature works celebrate the life of the rural working class in France in the nineteenth century. The son of a farmer, Millet was born in the peasant community of Gruchy on the Normandy coast. From a young age he showed an interest in art and was sent to study with a local portrait painter before entering the studio of an artist in provincial Cherbourg. He eventually went to Paris on a stipend awarded by the city of Cherbourg to study at the École des Beaux-Arts in the studio of history painter Paul Delaroche. Frustrated and unhappy there, Millet left the Academy in 1839 and moved back to Cherbourg the following year, where he established himself as a successful portraitist.

Washerwomen
about 1855
Oil on canvas
17 1/8 x 21 1/8 inches
Gift of Mrs. Martin Brimmer

In 1849, Millet moved to the town of Barbizon, on the edge of the Forest of Fontainebleau south of Paris, where he became acquainted with other artists working there, most notably Théodore Rousseau, who became his close friend. His mature works are a blend of the Barbizon ideals of landscape and the peasant life he had known since childhood. Millet sought to bring about working class reform through his work but his subjects, depicted with soft, luminous light, were as often romantic as they were socially thought-provoking. Despite this, Vincent van Gogh revered his work for its sensitive treatment of the rural working class.

Claude Monet
French, 1840–1926

Claude Monet was a leader of the group of painters who would become known in the nineteenth century as the Impressionists. The movement's name was derived from his 1873 painting titled *Impression: Sunrise*, which was shown in the group's first exhibition in 1874. He dedicated his life to painting the fleeting impressions of nature—those brief moments of atmospheric effects caused by the ever-changing movements of light and air. Monet was born in Paris but was raised in Le Havre on the Normandy coast. It was there, as a young man, that he met the painters Eugène Boudin and Johann Barthold Jongkind. Both men would play instrumental roles in Monet's formative years as a landscape artist, encouraging him to paint out-of-doors directly from nature while using vigorous brushwork that emphasized effects of color and light over topographical detail. In the early years of his career, Monet, like the other Impressionists, painted many scenes depicting human figures. As time went on, however, the landscape itself began to overtake his compositions.

Rue de la Bavolle, Honfleur
about 1864
Oil on canvas
22 x 24 inches
Bequest of John T. Spaulding

Following the death of his first wife Camille in 1879, Monet abandoned almost entirely the human subject. His life's work was marked by solitary travels throughout France and to distant locations such as Italy or Norway in search of new light and landscapes to paint from. In 1883, Monet moved to Giverny, about forty miles down the Seine from Paris, where he rented a house with a modest garden. In 1890 he bought the property and immediately set about expanding the grounds. In his later years, the garden at Giverny, with its extensive array of native and exotic plants and Japanese footbridge, served as the inspiration for nearly all of Monet's late works—images that have since become icons in the history of European art.

Left:
Meadow at Giverny
1886
Oil on canvas
36 1/4 x 32 1/8 inches
Juliana Cheney Edwards Collection

Right:
The Water Lily Pond
Japanese Bridge
1900
Oil on canvas
35 1/2 x 36 1/2 inches
Given in memory of Governor Alvan T. Fuller
by the Fuller Foundation

Camille Pissarro
French, 1830–1903

Camille Pissarro was born on the island of St. Thomas, then a Danish colony, into a Jewish family of French descent. His parents sent him to school in France in 1841, where he was instructed in drawing. In the 1850s he attended private classes at the École des Beaux-Arts and eventually enrolled at the Académie Suisse where he met Paul Cézanne and Claude Monet. Although he kept a studio in Paris he preferred to live in rural towns. During the 1860s he often painted with Camille Corot and also came under the influence of the Barbizon painter Charles-François Daubigny.

By the late 1860s, Pissarro had begun to align himself more closely with the group of artists he had met at the Académie Suisse who were reacting against the official Salon and establishing themselves as independents. He helped organize their first group show in 1874 and would continue to show with the Impressionist group until 1886—he was the only artist to participate in all eight of the group's exhibitions. Like Monet, he attempted to record the sensations he experienced in front of nature, but achieved little commercial success during his lifetime. Among the first collectors of his work were fellow artists such as Edgar Degas, Paul Gauguin, and Gustave Caillebotte. Today, the principal collection of Pissarro's paintings can be found at the Musée d'Orsay in Paris.

Pontoise, the Road to Gisors in Winter
1873
Oil on canvas
23 1/2 x 29 inches
Bequest of John T. Spaulding

View from the Artist's Window, Eragny
1885
Oil on canvas
21 7/16 x 25 5/8 inches
Juliana Cheney Edwards Collection

Pierre-Auguste Renoir

French, 1841–1919

Pierre-Auguste Renoir's career as an artist began when he was apprenticed to a painter of porcelain at the precocious age of 13. As he grew older he frequently visited the Louvre, perfecting his talents as a painter by copying the Old Masters. His mature style, marked by light, feathery brushstrokes and pastel colors, was heavily influenced by the eighteenth century French masters Jean Antoine Watteau, François Boucher, and Jean-Honoré Fragonard.

One of the founding members of the Impressionist group, Renoir met Claude Monet and Paul Cézanne while studying at the Académie Suisse in the 1860s. After participating in the first three Impressionist exhibitions, Renoir's style and choice of subject matter evolved from his decision to gain recognition through the official state-sponsored Salon. Following his great critical success at the Salon of 1879, Renoir continued to show works there. Cautious of alienating his new patrons he refused to exhibit in any more of the Impressionist exhibitions but remained close to his friends and their ideals. In the 1880s he traveled to Italy and northern Africa in search of new light effects before returning to the south of France to paint alongside his old friend Paul Cézanne. Throughout his career Renoir favored the sensuous curves of the female form. His figure paintings had a ready audience and were popular both in Europe and in America. The artist's last years were marked by poor health. Despite crippling rheumatism, which confined him to a wheelchair, Renoir never ceased working.

Woman with a Parasol and Small Child on a Sunlit Hillside
about 1874–76
Oil on canvas
18 1/2 x 22 1/8 inches
Bequest of John T. Spaulding

Left:
Children on the Seashore
about 1883
Oil on canvas
36 x 26 1/8 inches
Bequest of John T. Spaulding

Right:
Girls Picking Flowers in a Meadow
about 1890
Oil on canvas
25 5/8 x 31 7/8 inches
Juliana Cheney Edwards Collection

Théodore Rousseau
French, 1812–1867

Théodore Rousseau was a leader of the group of artists who settled in Barbizon, at the edge of the Forest of Fontainebleau, in the 1840s. His affinity for art and nature began as a schoolboy in Paris, where he made sketches of trees in the Bois de Boulogne. As early as the late 1820s Rousseau was painting from nature in the Forest of Fontainebleau. He had studied first with a cousin who introduced him to painting out-of-doors and later with two academic painters of history and historical landscape. Rousseau, however, was ill-suited for traditional landscape painting, which at that time required the introduction of mythological figures to "elevate" the subject. He preferred not to embellish his work but to faithfully represent nature as he encountered it. Rousseau would eventually become known, however, as "le grand refusé" for being systematically rejected by the Paris Salon between 1836 and 1841. The single landscape painter on the jury, a proponent of the classical approach to landscape painting, unfailingly rejected Rousseau. He would not return to the Salon again until after the revolution of 1848.

Pool in the Forest
Early 1850s
Oil on canvas
15 1/2 x 22 5/8 inches
Robert Dawson Evans Collection

Alfred Sisley
British, 1839–1899

Born in Paris to English parents, Alfred Sisley met Claude Monet and Auguste Renoir while studying in the studio of Charles Gleyre in the 1860s. Although one of the founding members of the Impressionist movement, Sisley never achieved the same level of notoriety as his comrades, despite reasonable commercial success later in life. In the 1870s, Sisley vigorously pursued landscape painting in towns around Paris such as Argenteuil and Louveciennes. In 1880, he moved to Moret-sur-Loing near the village of Saint-Mammès. Sisley wrote to Monet in 1881 describing the area as "not a bad spot, a bit of chocolate-box landscape" with "a very beautiful church and quite picturesque views." Despite the fact that writers and friends recognized Sisley's contribution to Impressionism during his lifetime, his contemporaries have overshadowed him in modern times.

Saint-Mammès: Morning (Le Matin)
1881
Oil on canvas
19 3/4 x 29 inches
Bequest of William A. Coolidge

The Loing at Saint-Mammès
1882
Oil on canvas
19 5/8 x 25 9/16 inches
Bequest of William A. Coolidge

Constant Troyon
French, 1810–1865

Considered one of the precursors of Impressionism, Constant Troyon was born in Sèvres, long a center for the production of porcelain in France. He received his first lessons in drawing from a porcelain painter and was later, like Auguste Renoir, employed as a porcelain decorator. After mediocre success exhibiting three landscapes at the Salon of 1833, he took up landscape painting in earnest and made several study trips to the French provinces. Through his friendship with Théodore Rousseau and other painters, he was encouraged to focus more on painting out-of-doors. Following contemporary fashion, he also took an interest in seventeenth century Dutch painting. In 1847, Troyon made a trip to the Netherlands where he encountered the animal paintings of Aelbert Cuyp and Paulus Potter. From that point forward animals became an integral element in his landscapes. The popularity of animal paintings in the nineteenth century guaranteed him a ready clientele throughout Europe. Demand for his work eventually became so great that he employed assistants to paint backgrounds so he could focus solely on painting animals.

Left:
Sheep and Shepherd in a Landscape
about 1854
Oil on canvas
13 3/4 x 17 3/4 inches
Bequest of Thomas Gold Appleton

Right:
Field Outside Paris
1845–51
Oil on paperboard
10 5/8 x 17 7/8 inches
The Henry C. and Martha B. Angell Collection

Antoine Vollon
French, 1833–1900

Antoine Vollon is probably best known as a painter of still-lifes and genre scenes. He began his career in the workshop of an enameller copying eighteenth century works for commercial use on decorative objects before attending the École des Beaux-Arts in Lyon. He moved to Paris in 1859 and began exhibiting at the Salon in 1864. He received numerous awards for his work and enjoyed a successful career as a state-sponsored artist. He also regularly sold his works to the French government. Vollon continued to exhibit at the Salon until 1880 and in 1897 was admitted as a member of the Académie des Beaux-Arts. Near the end of his life, he spent more time outside of Paris painting rural subjects out-of-doors. These late landscapes are not concerned with detail yet faithfully capture the subject with loose brushwork applied in quick, bold strokes.

Meadows and Low Hills
1867–69
Oil on panel
11 x 18 1/8 inches
Bequest of Ernest Wadsworth Longfellow

Select Bibliography

John Rewald, *Post-Impressionism from Van Gogh to Gauguin*, New York 1956

Gabriel Weisberg, *The Realist Tradition: French Painting and Drawing 1830-1900*, Cleveland 1980

Ronald Pickvance, *Van Gogh in St. Rémy and Auvers*, The Metropolitan Museum of Art 1984

Robert Rosenblum et al., *Art of the Nineteenth Century: Painting and Sculpture*, New York 1984

MaryAnne Stevens et al., *Alfred Sisley*, New Haven 1992

Steven Adams, *The Barbizon School & the Origins of Impressionism*, London 1994

John House et al., *Impressions of France: Monet, Renoir, Pissarro, and their Rivals*, The Museum of Fine Arts, Boston 1995

John Rewald, *Paintings of Paul Cézanne: A Catalogue Raisonné*, New York 1996

Bernard Denvir, *The Chronicle of Impressionism: An Intimate Diary of the Lives and World of the Great Artists*, New York 2000

George T.M. Shackelford, Fronia E. Wissman et al., *Impressions of Light: The French Landscape from Corot to Monet*, The Museum of Fine Arts, Boston 2002